Make Every Minute Count
Reinforcement Activities for Reading and Language Arts

Nicholas P. Criscuolo
Susan R. Fineman
Adrienne P. McCarthy

Scott, Foresman and Company
Glenview, Illinois   London

To Dr. Ted Forte — for his dedication
and commitment to effective teaching

 ® Good Year Books

are available for preschool through grade 12 and for every basic curriculum subject plus many enrichment areas. For more Good Year Books, contact your local bookseller or educational dealer.

For a complete catalog with information about other Good Year Books, please write:

Good Year Books
Department GYB
1900 East Lake Avenue
Glenview, Illinois 60025

Copyright © 1988 Scott, Foresman and Company.
All Rights Reserved.
Printed in the United States of America.
ISBN 0-673-18730-6

5678910 – BKC – 9291

No part of the book may be reproduced in any form or by any means, except those portions intended for classroom use, without permission in writing from the publisher.

PREFACE

"Every minute counts." Elementary teachers realize the importance of utilizing instructional time to the maximum degree. Despite the currently vogue concept of "prime time," in reality, every minute spent in the classroom is prime time.

Elementary teachers have always placed a high priority on the development of literacy — literacy enriches one's life, illiteracy diminishes it. Consequently, in daily classroom work, teachers strongly emphasize the acquisition of reading and language arts skills with their students.

Students not only acquire skills during the time allocated for the reading and language arts program, but also throughout the school day. One of the teacher's chief goals is to fully utilize available time, during the period designated "Before School," transitional periods and other times during the course of the school day. Unfortunately, some time often is wasted because the work assigned consists of meaningless, boring and unnecessary drills.

Crucial to a successful and effective reading/language arts program is emphasizing review and maintenance of skills. Such emphasis can be creatively accomplished through reinforcement activities that students can complete independently, without extensive guidance, since the skills covered have already been introduced. (Please note, however, that skills reinforcement does require *some* teacher direction and supervision.)

This book is designed to help elementary teachers searching for ways to involve children in a productive and worthwhile manner. Targeted for use in grades 2-4, the activities in this book are appropriate for children at all ability levels. All activities have been classroom-tested.

These activities are varied and have wide appeal for children. Some are open-ended while others require specific answers. They cover basic skills in reading and language arts and include such broad-based activities as completing puzzles, categorizing and completing sentences. Some activities sharpen comprehension skills, while others focus on writing through the use of story starters. As well, some activities include work with an encyclopedia, dictionary or newspaper.

All the worksheets contained in this book are designed for daily use. They encompass themes based on special areas of interest such as the community, entertainment, free time, mystery or sports. The activities in each section relate directly to one of the five themes. In addition, the level of difficulty varies with each section, allowing teachers to plan more efficiently for individual needs.

Another feature of these activities is that each worksheet activity is followed by a "Bonus" section. These bonus ideas are related to the main skill covered in each activity sheet and can be used for more than one day, or perhaps at a later time. This helps sustain enthusiasm while also enriching reading and language arts skills.

The activities have been designed to keep children productively occupied for a specified period of time. The directions for each activity are clearly stated, and suggested grade-level designations appear on the CONTENTS (By Skill) page.

A major benefit of this book is that these activities help children become independent learners (still, many activities may be adapted for small-group use). An answer key is included so teachers may make the activities both self-directing and self-correcting enterprises.

Make Every Minute Count contains creative ideas that not only reinforce important reading and language arts skills but also engender enthusiasm and interest on the part of the learner.

Nicholas P. Criscuolo, Ph.D.
Susan R. Fineman
Adrienne P. McCarthy

From *Make Every Minute Count,* Copyright © 1988 Scott, Foresman and Company

CONTENTS (By Title)

COMMUNITY
1. Fixing Up a Lot 1
2. Neighborhood Trip 2
3. Different Places 3
4. It Pays to Advertise 4
5. Signs Around Town 5
6. People, Places and Things 6
7. Parting Words 7
8. Under the Umbrella 8

ENTERTAINMENT
1. Enjoyable Decisions 9
2. Show Time 10
3. Picture Word Game 11
4. Day Trips 12
5. Let's Have a Party 13
6. A Way-Out Party 14
7. Changing Channels 15

FREE TIME
1. After School Fun 16
2. Rhyme Time 17
3. Pets Are People, Too! 18
4. Life's a Picnic 19
5. Charlie Goes to Camp 20
6. Search for Fun 21
7. Stamp It 22

MYSTERY
1. It's a Mystery to Me 23
2. Book Bags of Mystery 24
3. Sounds of Mystery 25
4. You Hold the Key 26
5. A Mysterious Plan 27
6. The Case of the Missing Prefix 28
7. Following Orders 29
8. Strange Happening 30

SPORTS
1. Dive Right In 31
2. Sporting Prefixes 32
3. A Sporting Life 33
4. Two in One 34
5. Strike Out 35
6. Swim Tryout 36
7. The Name of the Game 37
8. Take Aim 38

CONTENTS (By Skill)

COMMUNITY
1. Singular/Plural (3) 1
2. Blends (2) 2
3. Hard G/Soft G (3) 3
4. Long Vowels (2) 4
5. Short Vowels (3) 5
6. Long and Short Vowels (3-4) 6
7. Syllables (3) 7
8. Alphabetizing (3) 8

ENTERTAINMENT
1. Hard C/Soft C (3) 9
2. Contractions (3) 10
3. Compound Words (2) 11
4. Short Vowels (2) 12
5. Long and Short Vowels (2-3) 13
6. Base Words (4) 14
7. Synonyms (4) 15

FREE TIME
1. Contractions (2) 16
2. Rhyming Words (2) 17
3. Antonyms (3) 18
4. Homonyms (3-4) 19
5. Long Vowels (3) 20
6. Suffixes (2) 21
7. Guide Words (4) 22

MYSTERY
1. Singular/Plural (2) 23
2. Digraphs (2) 24
3. Irregular Vowels (3) 25
4. Antonyms (2-3) 26
5. Synonyms (3) 27
6. Prefixes (2) 28
7. Alphabetizing (4) 29
8. Guide Words (3) 30

SPORTS
1. Suffixes (3-4) 31
2. Prefixes (3-4) 32
3. Hard G/Soft G and Hard C/Soft C (3-4) 33
4. Compound Words (3-4) 34
5. Silent "e" (2) 35
6. Base Words (2-3) 36
7. Prefixes/Suffixes (4) 37
8. Homophones (4) 38

COMMUNITY

Your Name: _____

FIXING UP A LOT

NUMBER RIGHT ___
NUMBER WRONG ___

Write the plural for each word.

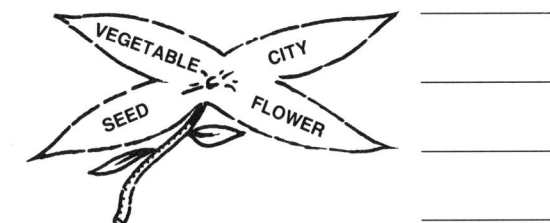   _____
                        _____
                        _____
                        _____

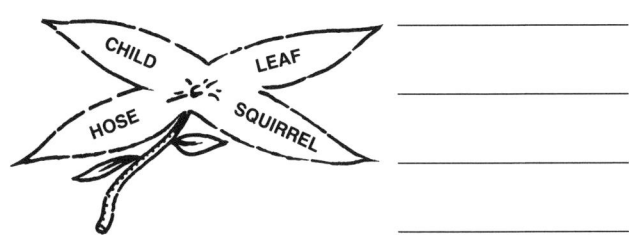   _____
                        _____
                        _____
                        _____

Write the singular for each word.

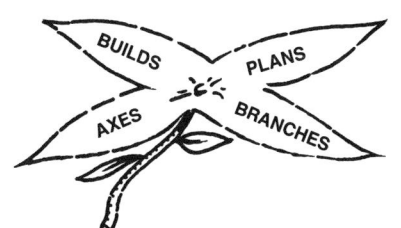   _____
                        _____
                        _____
                        _____

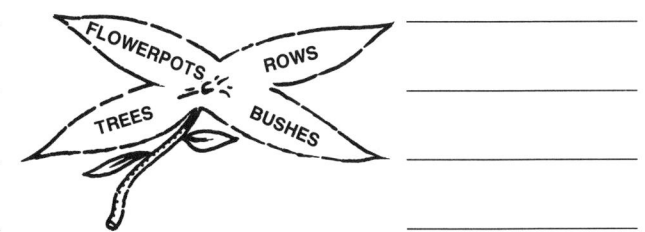   _____
                        _____
                        _____
                        _____

Read the story. Change each underlined word to either singular or plural.

Meg and Peter wanted to (1) <u>plants</u> a (2) <u>gardens</u> in an empty (3) <u>lots</u> at the end of their street. Both (4) <u>child</u> carried the (5) <u>tool</u> they would need — a (6) <u>rakes</u>, two (7) <u>shovel</u>, a (8) <u>hoses</u> and a pair of (9) <u>clipper</u>. Their father brought a power (10) <u>mowers</u> and an (11) <u>axes</u>. It took a lot of hard work, but little by little they cleared the lot and planted a beautiful (12) <u>gardens</u>.

(1) _____ (4) _____ (7) _____ (10) _____

(2) _____ (5) _____ (8) _____ (11) _____

(3) _____ (6) _____ (9) _____ (12) _____

 Draw a picture of the garden Meg and Peter planted.

SINGULAR/PLURAL

From *Make Every Minute Count,* Copyright © 1988 Scott, Foresman and Company

COMMUNITY

Your Name: _____

Fill in the blanks with the correct blend to complete each word.

On your <u>street</u>

1. Grows in a garden   (gl bl fl) __ __ ower
2. Cars on the road   (pr tr fr) __ __ affic
3. A toy in the yard   (bl gl sl) __ __ ide
4. Can carry big loads   (cr gr tr) __ __ uck
5. Someone you like   (pr fr gr) __ __ iend

At the <u>playground</u>

1. Fish swim in here   (br cr gr) __ __ ook
2. Will go higher and higher (tw dw sw) __ __ ing
3. Flies but cannot chirp   (bl cl pl) __ __ ane
4. Push with one foot   (sc sl st) __ __ ooter
5. Part of a tree   (fr gr br) __ __ anch

 Use all the "At the Playground" answers to draw a picture of a playground.

BLENDS

2   From *Make Every Minute Count,* Copyright © 1988 Scott, Foresman and Company

COMMUNITY

Your Name: _____

DIFFERENT PLACES

NUMBER RIGHT ___
NUMBER WRONG ___

All the words below begin with either a soft *g* sound or a hard *g* sound. Put each word in the SOFT G BOX or the HARD G BOX.

1. gerbil
2. gum
3. gold
4. giraffe
5. garlic
6. gingerbread
7. gorilla
8. goat

SOFT G BOX

HARD G BOX

 **BONUS** Where would you find each of the things listed in the boxes above? Put them under the correct place.

ZOO

STORE

HARD G/SOFT G

From *Make Every Minute Count*, Copyright © 1988 Scott, Foresman and Company

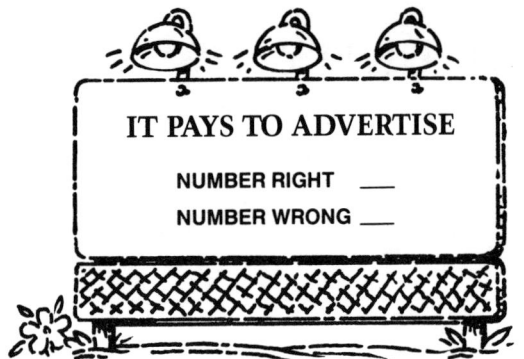

COMMUNITY

Your Name: _____

Blake's Grocery is having a sale on only long vowel items. Read the list below and circle each long vowel word. Then write the word on Blake's window.

| beef | fish | milk | cheese | grapes | bread | soap |
| jelly | eggs | rice | bleach | apples | ham | |

Bag your long vowel words in the correct vowel bag.

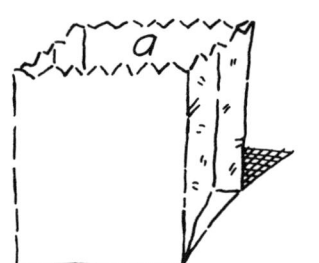   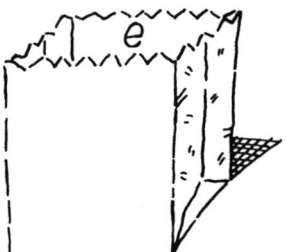   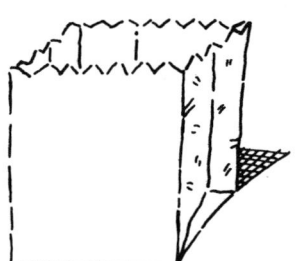   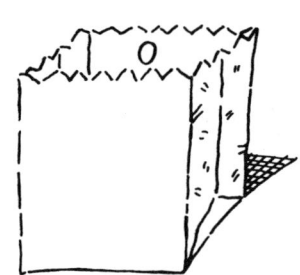

BONUS Make up your own ad about a sale on the following things.

FOR SALE

flute   paint   jeep

LONG VOWELS

COMMUNITY

Your Name: _____

SIGNS AROUND TOWN

NUMBER RIGHT ___
NUMBER WRONG ___

Read the sentences below. Choose only a *short* vowel word to complete each sentence. Then write the word next to the sign.

1. If you wanted to swim, you would go to the
   lake   beach   pond

2. If you wanted to go hiking, you would climb the
   mountain   cliff   earth

3. If you wanted to go on a trip, you would ride on the
   train   plane   bus

4. If you wanted to buy a model airplane kit, you would go to the
   craft shop   airport   art shop

5. If you wanted to buy some candy, you would go to the
   grocery store   food store   drug store

6. If you wanted to get rid of trash, you would go to the
   field   dump   yard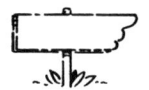

7. If you wanted to get across the river, you would go to the
   airport   bridge   water

8. If you wanted to see a haunted house, you would go to the
   shack   circus   fort

 Draw a map of a town. Include the eight places mentioned in the sentences above. Remember to label your map.

SHORT VOWELS

From *Make Every Minute Count*, Copyright © 1988 Scott, Foresman and Company

COMMUNITY

Your Name: _____

PEOPLE, PLACES AND THINGS

NUMBER RIGHT ___
NUMBER WRONG ___

Each word in the list below has a vowel sound underlined. Decide whether the sound is long or short. Then write the word in the correct column.

1. h<u>o</u>tel
2. f<u>e</u>nce
3. b<u>a</u>kery
4. cl<u>u</u>b
5. s<u>i</u>gns
6. t<u>a</u>xi
7. sw<u>i</u>ng
8. ph<u>o</u>ne
9. st<u>a</u>dium
10. gr<u>a</u>ss
11. s<u>i</u>dewalks
12. c<u>o</u>llege
13. p<u>e</u>ts
14. b<u>a</u>bies
15. p<u>o</u>liceman
16. st<u>a</u>tion
17. h<u>o</u>spital
18. tr<u>a</u>ffic
19. sl<u>i</u>de
20. tr<u>u</u>cks

LONG	SHORT

BONUS — On another piece of paper draw a map of a street that has a <u>bank</u>, <u>library</u>, <u>bakery</u>, and <u>hospital</u> on it. Label the buildings. Put in <u>sidewalks</u> and street <u>signs</u>.

LONG AND SHORT VOWELS

From *Make Every Minute Count,* Copyright © 1988 Scott, Foresman and Company

COMMUNITY

Your Name: _____

Read the words in the boxes below. Write each word under its correct heading. Then divide each word into syllables.

ambulance	illness
principal	teacher
deposit	savings
doctor	balcony
teller	gymnasium
actor	stagedoor

BANK

_____
_____
_____

HOSPITAL

_____
_____
_____

SCHOOL

_____
_____
_____

THEATER

_____
_____
_____

BONUS: On the back of this paper write the headings *Supermarket*, *Bakery* and *Library*. List *four* new words under each heading. Then divide each word into syllables.

SYLLABLES

From *Make Every Minute Count*, Copyright © 1988 Scott, Foresman and Company

COMMUNITY

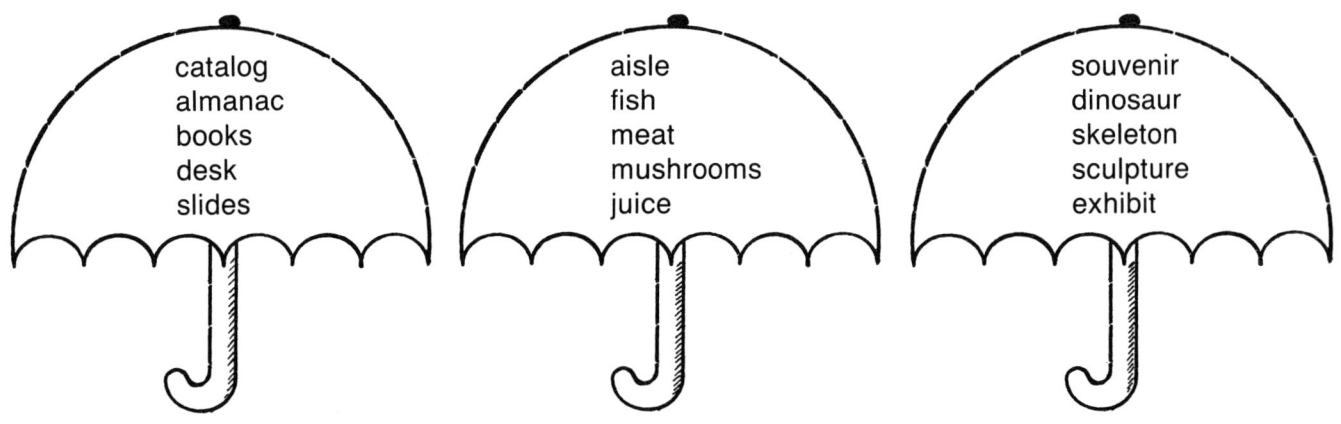

Your Name: _____

It's raining in every part of the city. In each umbrella there is a list of words. Put these words in alphabetical order under the name of the building in which you would most likely find them.

Umbrella 1: catalog, almanac, books, desk, slides

Umbrella 2: aisle, fish, meat, mushrooms, juice

Umbrella 3: souvenir, dinosaur, skeleton, sculpture, exhibit

MUSEUM
1. _____
2. _____
3. _____
4. _____
5. _____

LIBRARY
1. _____
2. _____
3. _____
4. _____
5. _____

SUPERMARKET
1. _____
2. _____
3. _____
4. _____
5. _____

Finish the alphabetical teams by writing in the missing letter.

d __ f   l __ n   g __ i   e __ g   r __ t

Write a word which begins with each missing letter and use it in a sentence.

ALPHABETICAL ORDER

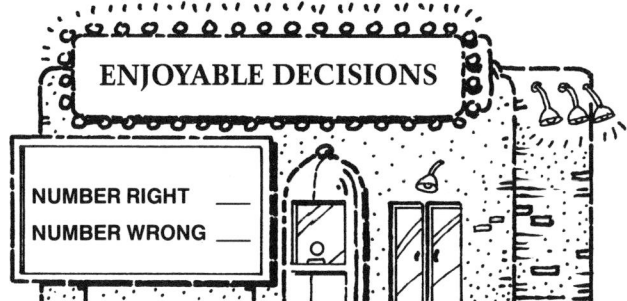

ENTERTAINMENT

Your Name: _____

Each word in the list below has either a soft *c* sound or a hard *c* sound. Decide whether the sound is soft or hard. Then write the word in the correct column.

	SOFT	HARD

1. camp
2. price
3. corral
4. race
5. cable
6. cabin
7. canvas
8. pace
9. taco
10. curtain
11. city
12. carrot
13. circus
14. license
15. canoe
16. comic
17. celebrate

Below are three things that will entertain you. Pick one of them and write a short story giving some reasons why it entertains you. In the story, be sure to use at least three hard *c* sounds and three soft *c* sounds. Underline these words.

radio

movie screen

record

HARD C/SOFT C

From *Make Every Minute Count*, Copyright © 1988 Scott, Foresman and Company

9

ENTERTAINMENT

Your Name: _____

Circle each pair of words that can be written as a contraction.

will it	that is
let us	could I
would not	are not
should we	have is

Write the contractions here:

_____ _____

_____ _____

Fill in each sentence with 2 contractions. Write out the two words that make up the contractions on the lines in the box at the end of each sentence.

CONTRACTION		TWO WORDS
wasn't I've	1. I _____ going to show our slides today but _____ changed my mind.	_____ _____ _____ _____
don't I'll	2. _____ bring some candy to the show. Why _____ you bring the buttered popcorn?	_____ _____ _____ _____
wouldn't We're	3. _____ showing slides of our trip to Florida. You _____ believe how many we have!	_____ _____ _____ _____
you'll I'm	4. _____ sure _____ be able to see everything if you sit on the sofa.	_____ _____ _____ _____
Shouldn't Let's	5. _____ your mother be here to help you run the projector? _____ call her in.	_____ _____ _____ _____

On another piece of paper, list 5 things that you might see in these slides of a Florida vacation. Draw a picture of 1 of these things.

CONTRACTIONS

ENTERTAINMENT

Your Name: _____

To play this game, circle the correct word to go with the picture that will make a compound word. Then write the compound word on the blank.

small
grand +  = _____
gold

        candle
        chocolate +  = _____
        pan

flash
bright +  = _____
dark

        water
        wooden +  = _____
        sail

ride
street +  = _____
red

        read
        note +  = _____
        library

buzz
honey +  = _____
bee

        dog
        good +  = _____
        back

What's your score? _____

On another piece of paper, make up your own compound words and pictures for your game. Play the game with a friend and see who gets the best score.

COMPOUND

From *Make Every Minute Count,* Copyright © 1988 Scott, Foresman and Company

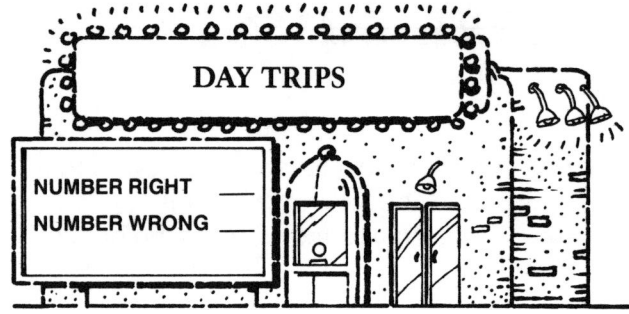

ENTERTAINMENT

Your Name: _____

Read each sentence. Circle the *short* vowel word under the sentence. Then write the word on the blank.

At the Circus

1. _____ funny clowns came out of a small car.
       Eight   Three   Six

2. The dancing horses had bright ribbons on their _____ .
       tails   legs   ears

3. We all laughed when the _____ jumped over the boxes.
       tramp   bear   clown

At the Farm

1. We had a great time swimming in the _____ .
       pool   pond   lake

2. Farmer Brown let me feed the _____ .
       sheep   goats   hens

3. Juan and I picked _____ beans in the garden.
       green   string   pole

At the Fair

1. There were good things to _____ at the fair.
       eat   see   drink

2. People liked to listen to the _____ .
       music   band   horns

3. Mom loved the _____ I won at the fair.
       book   cake   plant

BONUS

Which would you like to go to: a circus, a farm or a fair? Write your choice in a complete sentence on the line.

_____

Write two sentences about what you would see there.

SHORT VOWELS

From *Make Every Minute Count,* Copyright © 1988 Scott, Foresman and Company

ENTERTAINMENT

Your Name: _____

In the box below, find the *opposite* of each underlined word in the sentences. Write the word on the line. Then write [S] if the word you wrote has a *short* vowel sound. Write [L] if it has a *long* vowel sound.

| open | stay | bottom | left | sad | big | empty | light | dull | cold |

VOWEL SOUND

1. The birthday child is <u>happy</u>. _____ _____
2. Put my present on the <u>top</u>. _____ _____
3. The candy dish is <u>full</u>. _____ _____
4. Keep your eyes <u>closed</u>. _____ _____
5. The candles felt <u>hot</u>. _____ _____
6. The cake knife was <u>sharp</u>. _____ _____
7. Juan sat to my <u>right</u>. _____ _____
8. The toy is quite <u>little</u>. _____ _____
9. That box is so <u>heavy</u>. _____ _____
10. No one wanted to <u>leave</u>. _____ _____

Make a birthday wish. Draw a picture to show what that wish is.

LONG/SHORT VOWELS

From *Make Every Minute Count,* Copyright © 1988 Scott, Foresman and Company

ENTERTAINMENT

Your Name: _____

Read Jerry's party invitation below. Underline five words that have endings added to them. Write each word you find on the line. Then write the base word next to it.

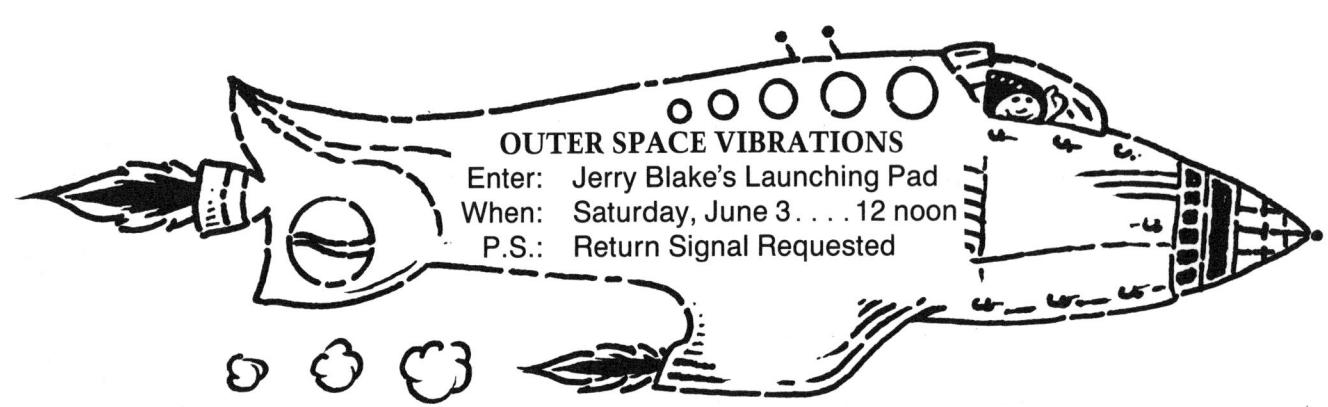

OUTER SPACE VIBRATIONS
Enter: Jerry Blake's Launching Pad
When: Saturday, June 3 .... 12 noon
P.S.: Return Signal Requested

        Word   **Base word**

1. _____ _____
2. _____ _____
3. _____ _____
4. _____ _____
5. _____ _____

Read Jerry's Moon Menu.
Underline eight words that have endings added to them. Then write the words you found below.

Moon Menu
Blast-off Burgers (Sloppy Joes)
Weightless Wafers (potato chips)
Milky Way Punch (chocolate milkshakes)

  Word   **Base word**   **Word**   **Base word**

1. _____ _____   5. _____ _____
2. _____ _____   6. _____ _____
3. _____ _____   7. _____ _____
4. _____ _____   8. _____ _____

Plan your own party invitation and menu. Choose one of the themes below. Circle your choice.

    Surprise Breakfast   Picnic for Two   Big Top Party

Now design your invitation and plan your menu. Invite your friends.

BASE WORDS

From *Make Every Minute Count,* Copyright © 1988 Scott, Foresman and Company

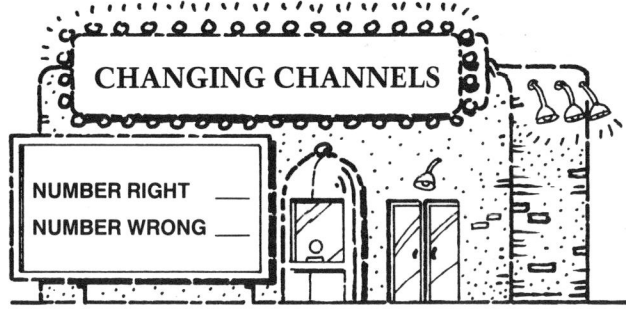

ENTERTAINMENT

Your Name: _____

Choose the correct synonym for each underlined word. Write the synonym on the blank. Use a dictionary if you need to.

9:00 AM	(2) America's Cup (mug, sauces) _____
	(4) Stop the Clock (go, halt) _____
	(6) Great Chefs of Europe (cooks, painters) _____
10:30 AM	(2) Let's Go to the Movies (television, theater) _____
	(4) The Young Doctor Miller (youthful, elderly) _____
	(6) Journey into Space (trek, time) _____
11:30 AM	(2) History of Jesters (teachers, clowns) _____
	(4) Wild Animals (untamed, tamed) _____
	(6) Show Your Strength (hide, exhibit) _____
1:00 PM	(2) Name that Melody (person, tune) _____
	(4) The Art of Aviation (photography, flying) _____
	(6) A Banquet for Kings (weapon, feast) _____

Choose your favorite program from the listings above. Write six or more sentences telling about the program.

SYNONYMS

From *Make Every Minute Count,* Copyright © 1988 Scott, Foresman and Company

FREE TIME

Your Name: _____

Circle the contraction that makes sense in the sentence. Write it on the blank.

1. _____ my new bike.   That's   Isn't
2. _____ make a snowman.   Hadn't   Let's
3. _____ he want to skate?   Doesn't   Hasn't
4. We _____ go to the zoo.   haven't   can't
5. Tom _____ in our club.   isn't   I'm
6. _____ get the sled.   I'll   That's
7. We _____ find the jacks.   couldn't   doesn't
8. Why _____ we skip home?   don't   doesn't

Circle the sentence above that you like best.
Write the sentence on another piece of paper.
Draw a picture about your sentence.

CONTRACTIONS

16 From *Make Every Minute Count,* Copyright © 1988 Scott, Foresman and Company

FREE TIME

Your Name: _____

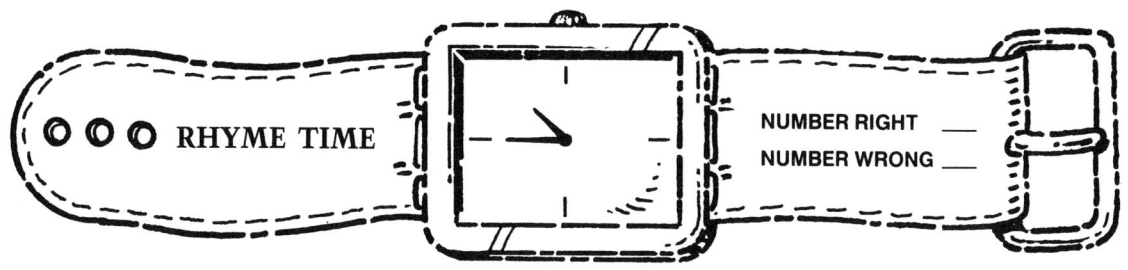

RHYME TIME

NUMBER RIGHT ___
NUMBER WRONG ___

Find three rhyming words in each box. Write them on the blanks. Then complete each sentence.

boy	hay	day
pay	toy	Roy
say	way	soy

_____

_____

_____

Will you ask the _____

if I can use his _____ car?

wake	cake	hike
fake	like	bake
bike	mike	lake

_____

_____

_____

Would you _____ to _____

along a forest trail?

look	moon	brook
book	noon	hook
cook	took	soon

_____

_____

_____

Which _____ will you _____

in to find out what hamsters eat?

Write four words that rhyme with: bat   tent   game

RHYMING WORDS

From *Make Every Minute Count*, Copyright © 1988 Scott, Foresman and Company

17

FREE TIME

Your Name: _____

NUMBER RIGHT ___
NUMBER WRONG ___

Read the following story.

　　One warm day, a dog named Barky was playing ball with a tall boy named John. After about an hour, Barky felt tired. Together Barky and John went inside their house and had some delicious milk. Just then Barky slowly looked back over his shoulder. He saw his tail wagging and he started to cry. "What's the matter, Barky?" asked John. "My tail!" said Barky. "It moves back and forth when I'm happy." John began to laugh. "Your tail is supposed to move!" shouted John. "But, why?" asked Barky. "So your owner knows when you are happy," replied John, still smiling.

Write each underlined word next to its antonym.

before　　_____　　　under　　_____

outside　　_____　　　short　　_____

front　　_____　　　cry　　_____

laugh　　_____　　　bad-tasting _____

rapidly　　_____　　　sad　　_____

whispered _____　　　rested　　_____

ended　　_____　　　cool　　_____

frowning _____　　　apart　　_____

What's your favorite kind of pet? Write a story about what you would do if someone gave you three of them.

ANTONYMS

18　　　　From *Make Every Minute Count,* Copyright © 1988 Scott, Foresman and Company

FREE TIME

Your Name: _____

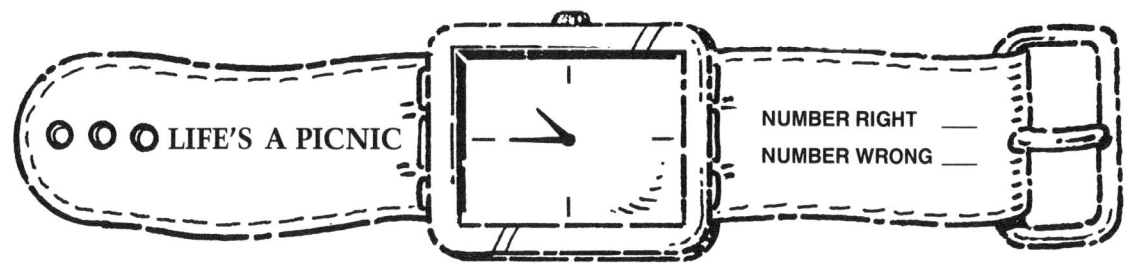

NUMBER RIGHT ___
NUMBER WRONG ___

Write the correct word on the blank in each sentence. Then, check *YES* or *NO*.

pair / pear	1. Life's a picnic. Have you ever eaten a _____ at one?
four / for	2. Life's a book. Have you ever bought one _____ a friend?
rows / rose	3. Life's a flower. Have you ever smelled a yellow _____ ?
no / know	4. Life's a skateboard. Do you _____ how to balance on one?
won / one	5. Life's a game. Have you ever _____ a coloring contest?
bear / bare	6. Life's a bike. Have you ever taken a ride in your _____ feet?
write / right	7. Life's a song. Have you ever tried to _____ one?
Would / Wood	8. Life's a friend. _____ you be happy playing with one?

YES / NO

Make up your own sayings. Use *one* of the two words in front of each sentence.

high / hi	1. Life's a *kite*. _____ ?
eight / ate	2. Life's a _____ . _____ ?
sale / sail	3. Life's a _____ . _____ ?

YES / NO

Use another piece of paper. Draw a large t-shirt. Choose one of the sayings above and put it, along with a picture, on the shirt.

HOMONYMS

From *Make Every Minute Count*, Copyright © 1988 Scott, Foresman and Company

FREE TIME

Your Name: _____

Read the letter below. Choose four long vowel words from each day. Circle the long vowel words, then write them on the blanks.

Dear Mom,

Monday: Our cabin is very tiny. The food is not too good. But my new friend, Pete, is great. Tomorrow our swim lessons start. Camp is fun!

_____   _____   _____   _____

Tuesday: Guess what? Someone pushed me in the lake. That's how the swim lesson started. Don't worry — all went well. Wednesday, the campers will hike up Mount Aspic.

_____   _____   _____   _____

Wednesday: Boy, what a trip! It took us four hours to climb up the mountain. One camper got lost and a plane had to search for him. Paul was found sitting near a stream. His leg was broken. What next?

_____   _____   _____   _____

Thursday: Well, Mom, it poured all day. Our cabin got soaked and sank into the mud. All of us had to move to another place. Can anything else happen? Let's hope not!

_____   _____   _____   _____

Love,
Charlie

Write what Charlie might have done Friday, Saturday and Sunday at camp.

LONG VOWELS

From *Make Every Minute Count,* Copyright © 1988 Scott, Foresman and Company

FREE TIME

Your Name: _____

Read the words in the box. Find the words in the puzzle. Look ←--→ and ↕. Circle each word.

WORD BOX

RECORD
FINISH
FISH
PRETEND
PAINT
MEET
STRETCH
CATCH
WASH
READ
WEAR
TICKET

F	W	N	W	T	B	L	C
I	E	P	A	I	N	T	R
S	A	R	S	C	C	R	E
H	R	E	H	K	A	E	N
I	S	T	R	E	T	C	H
M	E	E	T	T	C	O	A
F	I	N	I	S	H	R	E
O	M	D	R	E	A	D	L

Add *s, es, ed* or *ing*, to each underlined word.

1. Sometimes Dad takes me fish (_____).

2. They pretend (_____) to be riding in a spaceship.

3. I enjoy read (_____) books about wild animals.

4. Three girls paint (_____) pictures on the long roll of paper.

5. Alison will be wear (_____) a clown suit to the party.

6. My sister won three ticket (_____) to the circus.

7. Mark is wash (_____) his car in the parking lot.

8. Bonnie finish (_____) sewing the doll's clothes last night.

Draw a picture of one of the sentences. Put yourself in the drawing.

SUFFIXES

From *Make Every Minute Count*, Copyright © 1988 Scott, Foresman and Company

FREE TIME

Your Name: _____

Read the sentences and look at the GUIDE WORD BOX. In the blank after each sentence write the pair of guide words that the underlined word comes between.

GUIDE WORD BOX
antique – any
punish – purple
ranch – rash
position – post
vase – vein
attain – attire
crow – cruelty
formal – forum
respect – rest
vapor – vary
hug – humor
neat – needle
fatigue – feast
expand – explain
plaza – pledge

1. Stamp collecting is my favorite hobby. _____
2. My collection of stamps is vast. _____
3. I attend many stamp shows with my friend. _____
4. The stamp shows are always crowded. _____
5. It is not expensive to attend these shows. _____
6. At these shows, I look for rare stamps. _____
7. Sometimes I am fortunate to find such stamps. _____
8. When I do, I purchase them. _____
9. The stamps come in various sizes. _____
10. I paste the stamps in a huge stamp book. _____
11. I only need a few stamps to fill one book. _____
12. I also respond to ads in stamp magazines. _____
13. I possess stamps from many countries. _____
14. I am anxious to increase my collection. _____
15. Stamp collecting gives me many hours of pleasure. _____

Below are stamps from two countries. Read the words under each country and draw a picture of it.

SWITZERLAND
Alps Mountains

EGYPT
Pyramid

GUIDE WORDS

NUMBER RIGHT ___
NUMBER WRONG ___

IT'S A MYSTERY TO ME

MYSTERY

Your Name: _____

Write *S* in front of a singular word. Then write the plural of the word. Write *P* in front of a plural word. Then write the singular of the word.

____ footstep _____   ____ monsters _____

____ robbers _____   ____ clues _____

____ scare _____   ____ skeletons _____

____ spy _____   ____ ghost _____

CROSS OUT THE PLURAL WORDS

flashlight	witches	captures	mysteries
flashlights	witch	capture	mystery

CROSS OUT THE SINGULAR WORDS

graves	shadow	fingerprint	bones
grave	shadows	fingerprints	bone

In the following sentences, use ⑤ of the words not crossed out above.

1. The skeleton's _____ hung in the closet.

2. Use the _____ when you go down those dark cellar stairs!

3. The _____ of the tall oak trees made the old house look spooky.

4. Some people believe that a _____ lives in that old cave.

5. Who do you think will _____ the man who robbed the bank?

BONUS

Write the ③ words that you did not use.

_____ _____ _____

Put each word in a scary sentence.

SINGULAR/PLURAL

From *Make Every Minute Count,* Copyright © 1988 Scott, Foresman and Company   23

MYSTERY

Your Name: _____

Read the following titles of mystery books. Choose the correct digraph to complete the word. Circle the digraph, then write it on the blank.

1. The Case of the Missing __ __ ief

    Sh   Th   Wh

2. A Haunted __ __ ack

    Wh   Th   Sh

3. Magic Mountain's Wit __ __

    ch   sh   th

4. Lost in a __ __ eat Field

    Th   Wh   Sh

5. The Spy in the Chur __ __

    sh   ch   th

6. A Clue Found on the Pa __ __

    wh   sh   th

7. Master of Bea __ __ Castle

    sh   ch   wh

8. A __ __ adow in the Night

    Th   Ch   Sh

9. The __ __ ale Who Saved a Boy

    Ch   Wh   Th

10. The Giant with the Gold Too __ __

    sh   wh   th

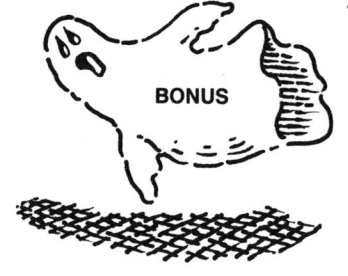

Think of a title for a mystery story. Then draw a poster about your book.

DIGRAPHS

MYSTERY

Your Name: _____

Underneath each mystery book title are phrases with an irregular vowel sound. Circle the word with the irregular vowel sound. Then underline one word with the same sound as the circled word.

THE HIDDEN TREASURE

along the brook	book	soon
the wrinkled shirt	heave	circle
soot in the trunk	soon	took
a short man	pork	from
a bag of wool	hood	tool

THE ANIMAL CAGE

the missing paw	crawl	mask
thick piece of wood	worm	stood
turn of the head	curve	stand
the huge broom	tall	toot
an autumn night	boot	auction

THE HAUNTED HOUSE

the hidden claw	clay	paw
a slow step	load	clear
an awful grin	mop	jaw
grasped the sore hand	more	pool
absent from the group	mound	loot

Pick one of the mystery books. Use the phrases in that book to write your own mystery story.

IRREGULAR VOWELS

From *Make Every Minute Count,* Copyright © 1988 Scott, Foresman and Company

MYSTERY

NUMBER RIGHT ___
NUMBER WRONG ___

YOU HOLD THE KEY

Your Name: _____

Follow the path to the key. Write each word along the path next to its antonym.

Path words: scream, nervous, alive, run, questions, uncover, shaky, foggy, exciting, dangerous, caught, unusual

Antonyms:

_____ COVER   _____ ANSWERS

_____ CALM   _____ NORMAL

_____ BORING   _____ CLEAR

_____ WALK   _____ DEAD

_____ RELEASED   _____ SAFE

_____ STEADY   _____ WHISPER

Fill in the sentences with a pair of antonyms from the list above.

1. Going into that haunted house made me so _____ I couldn't _____ down for an hour!

2. Although the road looked _____ , there was a _____ curve near the hidden cave.

3. Even though things appear _____ , something very _____ is going on around here!

BONUS

What do you think the key opens? Write a story about it.

ANTONYMS

26   From *Make Every Minute Count,* Copyright © 1988 Scott, Foresman and Company

MYSTERY

NUMBER RIGHT ___
NUMBER WRONG ___

Your Name: _____

Circle the synonym for each underlined word.

1. The thief wanted to steal a treasure map from the King.　　　(robber, policeman, ghost)

2. He knew he would need his hatchet to chop down an old wooden door at the back of the castle.　　　(mask, rope, ax)

3. Just as he started out on his journey, he remembered something else.　　　(fingerprints, bicycle, trip)

4. He reached for his cleaver, sharpened its blade, and left for the castle.　　　(pencil, candle, knife)

5. As the thief walked through the woods, the moon cast gloomy shadows on his path.　　　(funny, thin, dark)

6. Running through a cemetery, he tripped over a wooden box that looked like a casket.　　　(coffin, bush, fence)

7. Suddenly, he heard a strange moan, or cry, coming from inside the box.　　　(laugh, sob, squeak)

8. Trembling, he wondered if the sounds could be those of a ghost, or goblin.　　　(nest, wall, spirit)

BONUS

You finish the story. Choose your own ending. Write your ending on a separate piece of paper.

SYNONYMS

From *Make Every Minute Count,* Copyright © 1988 Scott, Foresman and Company

NUMBER RIGHT ___
NUMBER WRONG ___

THE CASE OF THE MISSING PREFIX

MYSTERY

Your Name: _____

Read the following story about a robbery. Complete each sentence by choosing the correct word from the chest. Write it on the blank.

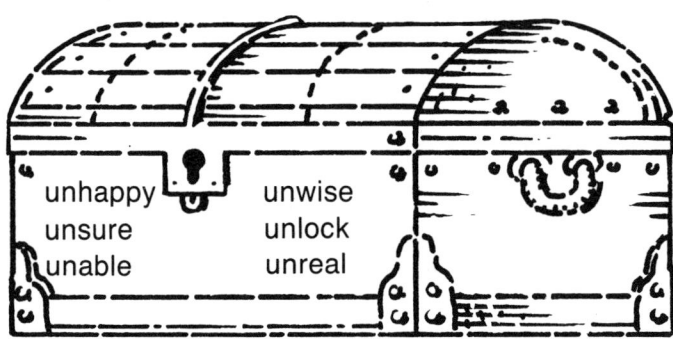

unhappy   unwise
unsure   unlock
unable   unreal

1. Someone tried to _____ the chest.

2. We are _____ of how the robber got into the house.

3. The police were _____ to find any clues.

4. The robber should know it is _____ to steal.

5. Dad cannot believe this happened. It seems so _____ .

6. Our family feels very _____ about the robbery.

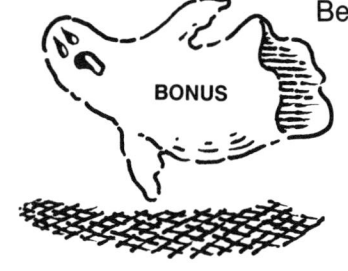

BONUS

Be a good detective and write one word with each of the prefixes below.

1. re _____   2. un _____   3. mis _____   4. dis _____

Use each word in a sentence.

1. _____

2. _____

3. _____

4. _____

PREFIXES

28   From *Make Every Minute Count,* Copyright © 1988 Scott, Foresman and Company

MYSTERY

NUMBER RIGHT ___
NUMBER WRONG ___

FOLLOWING ORDERS

Your Name: _____

Number each list of words to show alphabetical order. Then, write your alphabetized list on the lines.

LIST A

- ☐ magical   __magic__
- ☒ 1 magic   _____
- ☐ mummy   _____
- ☐ mysterious   _____
- ☐ murder   _____
- ☐ mystical   _____

LIST B

- ☐ Frankenstein _____
- ☐ frighten _____
- ☐ foggy _____
- ☐ footprints _____
- ☐ fright _____
- ☐ footsteps _____

LIST C

- ☐ ghostly _____
- ☐ grave _____
- ☐ getaway _____
- ☐ grabs _____
- ☐ glowing _____
- ☐ gloomy _____

LIST D

- ☐ skeleton _____
- ☐ spirits _____
- ☐ search _____
- ☐ spies _____
- ☐ spooky _____
- ☐ shadow _____

BONUS

Write a scary story using at least eight of the words above.

ALPHABETIZING

From *Make Every Minute Count,* Copyright © 1988 Scott, Foresman and Company

MYSTERY

NUMBER RIGHT ___
NUMBER WRONG ___

Your Name: _____

Read the following story. After some words there is a line. On the line write the number that matches the guide words in the box below.

Rita always looked forward to spending her summer vacation with Aunt Viola. She enjoyed the journey _____ to Aunt Viola's farm. There she had the opportunity _____ to milk the cows and feed the chickens. She also liked picking blueberries in the blueberry patch _____ near Aunt Viola's house.

It was a sad day for Rita because she had to return _____ home. Aunt Viola drove her to the railroad station. Rita walked up to the window and purchased _____ a ticket. She waited on the platform for her train to arrive _____ .

As Rita was waiting, a man in a tattered _____ suit came up to her. He handed her a package. Rita tried to speak to him, but he fled _____ .

Rita heard a ticking sound coming from the package. She ran up to a policeman. The policeman took the package and said, "That man likes to play jokes. All there is in this package is an alarm clock!"

1. arm – arrow	5. tasty – tea
2. oppose – ordinary	6. job – judgment
3. party – paste	7. flat – fleece
4. retire – reveal	8. punish – purr

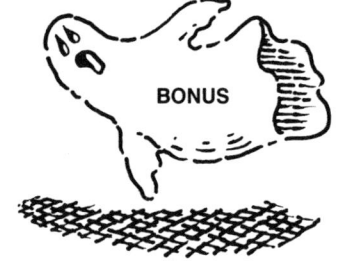

BONUS

Below are a suitcase and a trunk. Both have guide words in them. Choose one, and use as many guide words from it as you can to write a mysterious story.

eerie – find
goblin – ghost
haunted – have
hidden – hive
shadow – shake

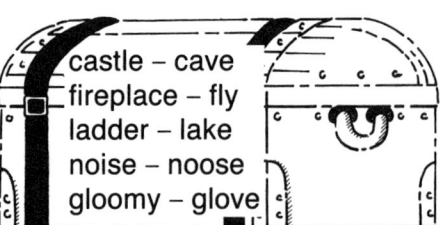

castle – cave
fireplace – fly
ladder – lake
noise – noose
gloomy – glove

GUIDE WORDS

30 From *Make Every Minute Count,* Copyright © 1988 Scott, Foresman and Company

SPORTS

DIVE RIGHT IN

SCOREBOARD

NUMBER RIGHT ___

NUMBER WRONG ___

Your Name: _____

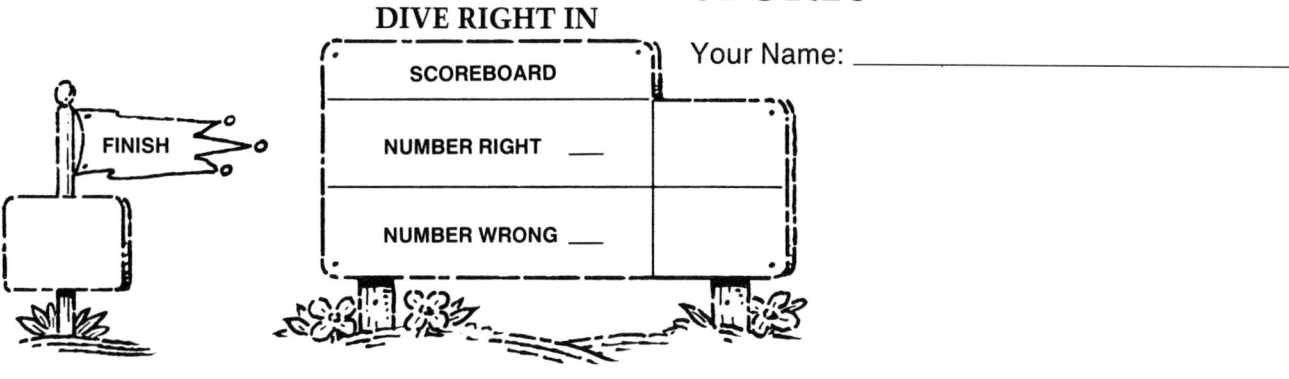

Add one of the suffixes in the box to the word below the line in each sentence. Write the new word on the line.

| ize, ible, ish, ful, ance, ous, ment |

1. The swimmer's _____ was almost perfect.
   (perform)

2. Winning this event was a major _____ .
   (accomplish)

3. You must be _____ to do a split in the air.
   (flex)

4. A backwards dive can be very _____ .
   (danger)

5. _____ at the swimming events was high.
   (Attend)

6. A diver tries to _____ his dive before doing it.
   (visual)

7. The contestant was _____ . She didn't want
   (care)
   to slip on the diving board.

8. Before diving, _____ your weight as you jump.
   (equal)

9. You could feel the _____ of the crowd.
   (excite)

10. That last dive looked a bit _____ .
    (amateur)

BONUS

List as least 6 sporting events that take place during the Olympics. Tell which is your favorite event and why.

SUFFIXES

From *Make Every Minute Count*, Copyright © 1988 Scott, Foresman and Company

SPORTS

SPORTING PREFIXES

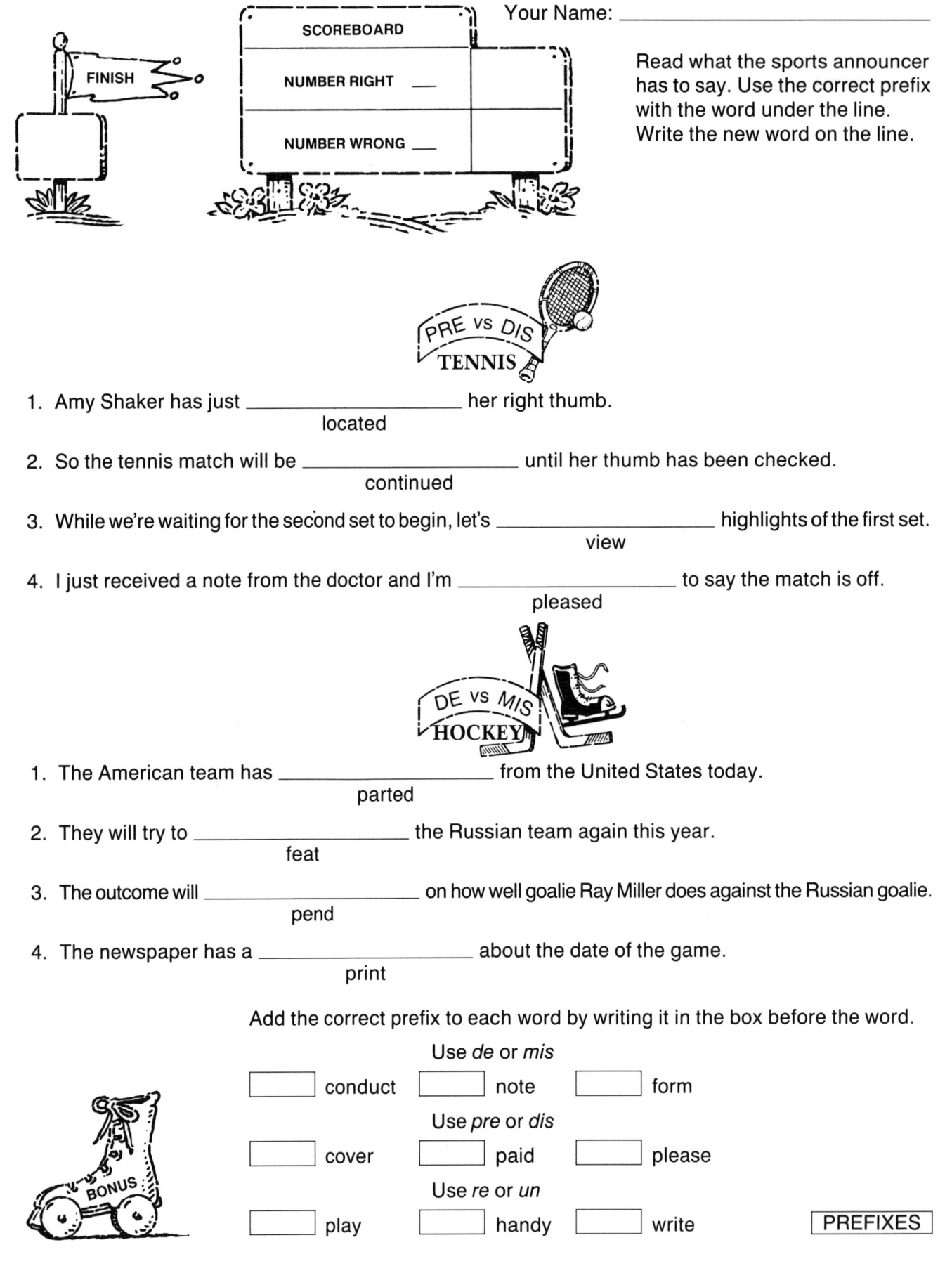

Your Name: _____

SCOREBOARD
NUMBER RIGHT ___
NUMBER WRONG ___

Read what the sports announcer has to say. Use the correct prefix with the word under the line. Write the new word on the line.

PRE vs DIS — TENNIS

1. Amy Shaker has just _____ her right thumb.
                                 located

2. So the tennis match will be _____ until her thumb has been checked.
                                       continued

3. While we're waiting for the second set to begin, let's _____ highlights of the first set.
                                                                   view

4. I just received a note from the doctor and I'm _____ to say the match is off.
                                                                                  pleased

DE vs MIS — HOCKEY

1. The American team has _____ from the United States today.
                                   parted

2. They will try to _____ the Russian team again this year.
                                   feat

3. The outcome will _____ on how well goalie Ray Miller does against the Russian goalie.
                                   pend

4. The newspaper has a _____ about the date of the game.
                                   print

Add the correct prefix to each word by writing it in the box before the word.

Use *de* or *mis*

☐ conduct   ☐ note   ☐ form

Use *pre* or *dis*

☐ cover   ☐ paid   ☐ please

Use *re* or *un*

☐ play   ☐ handy   ☐ write

PREFIXES

SPORTS

A SPORTING LIFE

Your Name: _____

SCOREBOARD

NUMBER RIGHT ___

NUMBER WRONG ___

Look at the words under the tennis court and the basketball court. If the word has a soft *c* or *g* sound, write it below the tennis court. If it has a hard *c* or *g* sound, write it below the basketball.

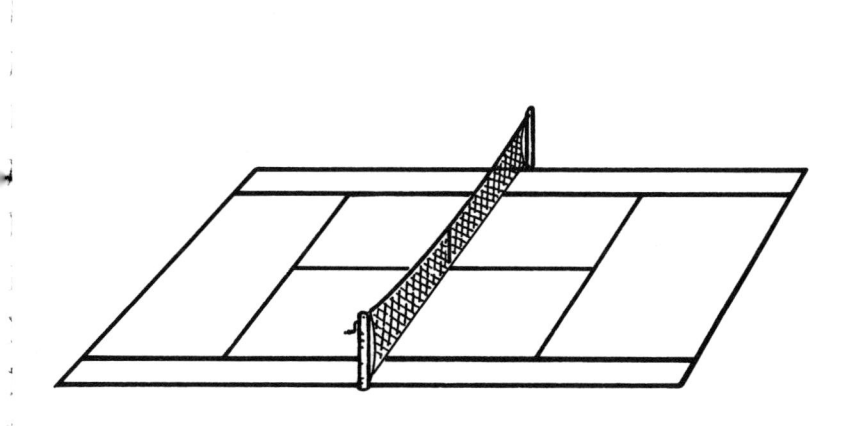

1. catcher   2. receiver   3. slice   4. golf   5. singles
6. center   7. gymnasium   8. ace   9. canoe   10. advantage

Write two words with a soft *g* sound and two with a hard *g* sound. Do the same for the hard and soft *c* sound. Use all eight words in a sports story.

HARD G/SOFT G and HARD C/SOFT C

From *Make Every Minute Count*, Copyright © 1988 Scott, Foresman and Company

SPORTS

TWO IN ONE

SCOREBOARD

NUMBER RIGHT ___

NUMBER WRONG ___

Your Name: _____

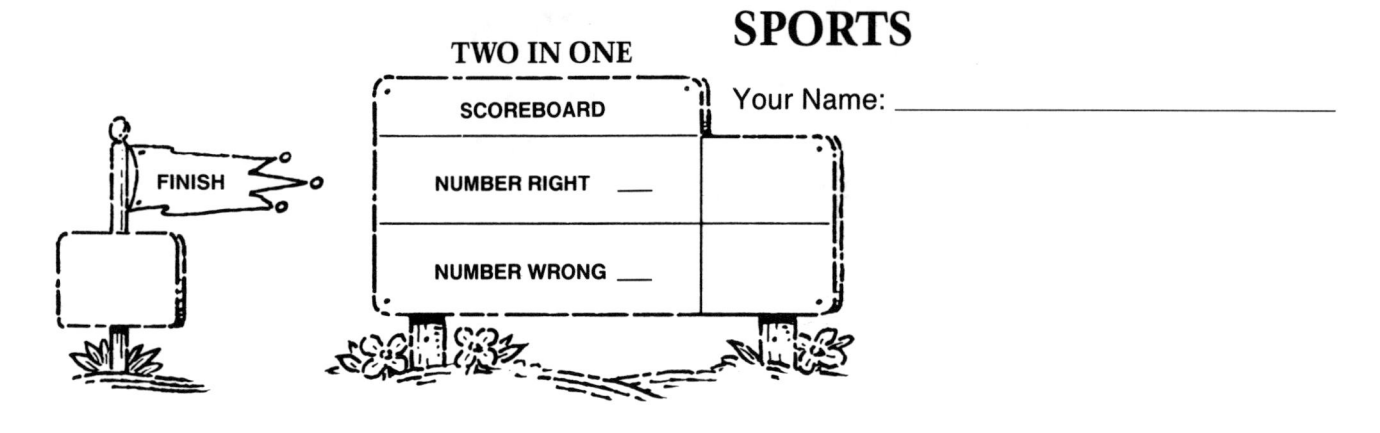

Draw a line connecting two words to make a compound word. Write the compound word on the line.

grand	board
score	shoe
horse	stand

_____
_____
_____

racquet	board
skate	ball
mountain	side

_____
_____
_____

flag	post
gate	pole
quarter	back

_____
_____
_____

Find one compound word in each sentence below. Circle the word. Then, fill in each blank using one of the words from the *above* list.

1. A blacksmith made these.   _____

2. Hoofprints were found here.   _____

3. It is a starting place at a racetrack.   _____

4. His picture was in the newspaper.   _____

BONUS

You are jogging in your neighborhood. On the back of this paper, list the names of at least six people or places you see. List only compound words.

COMPOUND WORDS

34   From *Make Every Minute Count,* Copyright © 1988 Scott, Foresman and Company

SPORTS

STRIKE OUT

SCOREBOARD

NUMBER RIGHT ___

NUMBER WRONG ___

Your Name: _____

Read each word below. Strike out the silent *e*. Check *Yes* if a new word is made. Check *No* if a new word is not made. If a new word is made, write it on the line.

Word	Yes	No	New Word
1. bite	☐	☐	bit
2. shake	☐	☐	_____
3. plane	☐	☐	_____
4. blade	☐	☐	_____
5. note	☐	☐	_____
6. plume	☐	☐	_____
7. huge	☐	☐	_____
8. spine	☐	☐	_____
9. mope	☐	☐	_____
10. slide	☐	☐	_____
11. paste	☐	☐	_____
12. stripe	☐	☐	_____

BONUS

Add an *e* to each word. On the back of this paper, draw a picture of each new word.

cub ___   kit ___

rob ___   tub ___

dim ___   cap ___

SILENT E

From *Make Every Minute Count,* Copyright © 1988 Scott, Foresman and Company

SPORTS

SWIM TRYOUT

SCOREBOARD

NUMBER RIGHT ___

NUMBER WRONG ___

Your Name: _____

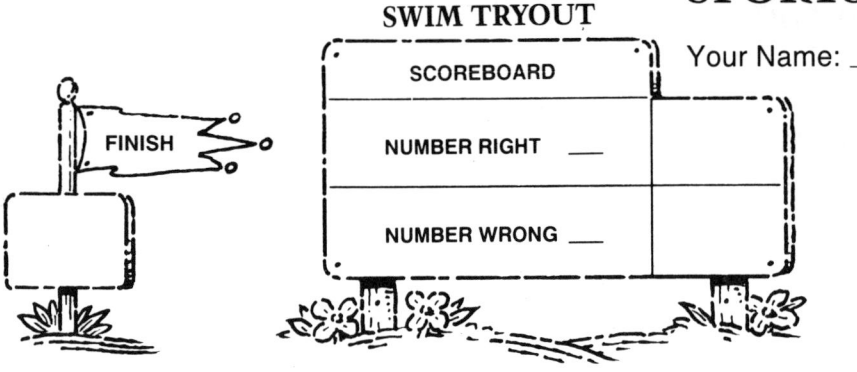

Read the story below. Underline twenty words that have endings added to them. Then write the *base words* on the lines.

    Stephanie was interested in becoming a member of the school swim team. She practiced her strokes everyday in the swimming pool. The backstroke seemed to be the easiest for her to learn. She worked hardest at diving. Stephanie tried to improve each day in hopes of making the team. At last, the list of names were posted. Much to her disappointment, Stephanie did not see her name on the list. Then, she heard her name called over the loud speaker. She went to the office and saw Coach Wall standing by the door. He explained to her why her name was not on the list. It was his mistake . . . he wrote the name Stephan instead of Stephanie.

Base Words

1. _____   6. _____   11. _____   16. _____
2. _____   7. _____   12. _____   17. _____
3. _____   8. _____   13. _____   18. _____
4. _____   9. _____   14. _____   19. _____
5. _____   10. _____   15. _____   20. _____

Write the name of the sport you like best on the line below.

_____

Now list four words that tell about your sport. Add endings to each base word you choose.

1. _____
2. _____
3. _____
4. _____

BASE WORDS

From *Make Every Minute Count,* Copyright © 1988 Scott, Foresman and Company

THE NAME OF THE GAME

SPORTS

SCOREBOARD

NUMBER RIGHT ___

NUMBER WRONG ___

Your Name: _____

Draw a circle around the prefix in the words next to each sports picture. **Draw** a line under the suffix.

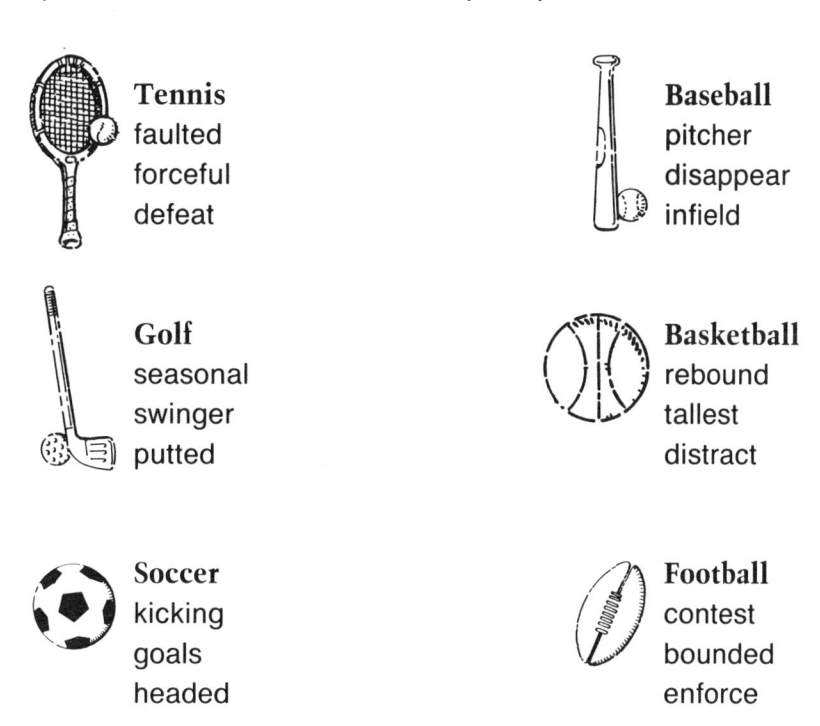

Tennis
faulted
forceful
defeat

Baseball
pitcher
disappear
infield

Golf
seasonal
swinger
putted

Basketball
rebound
tallest
distract

Soccer
kicking
goals
headed

Football
contest
bounded
enforce

On the line after each word, write the name of the sport that is associated with the words below.

hoop _____

tee _____

puck _____

mitt _____

gloves _____

shoulder pads _____

PREFIXES AND SUFFIXES

From *Make Every Minute Count*, Copyright © 1988 Scott, Foresman and Company   37

SPORTS

TAKE AIM

SCOREBOARD
NUMBER RIGHT ___
NUMBER WRONG ___

Your Name: _____

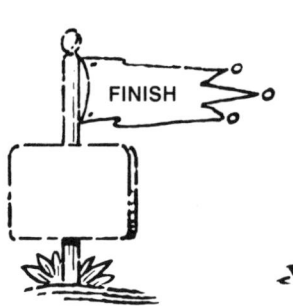

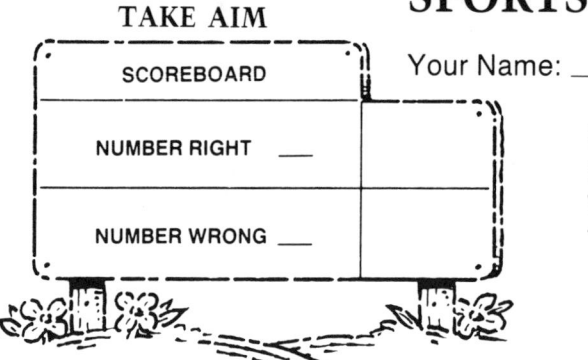

Find the word in the WORD BOX to complete each sentence. Write the word on the line. Then put it in the maze.

WORD BOX

paws	pause
steel	steal
by	buy
through	threw
main	mane
pale	pail
break	brake
daze	days

1. Harold used his own money to _____ fifty dollars worth of sporting equipment.

2. The ball player was in a _____ after getting hit in the head with the ball.

3. After a brief _____ , the shooter took aim.

4. James _____ the ball too hard. The referee called a foul.

5. If David makes this point, he'll _____ the tie.

6. The _____ reason Jennifer scores so many points is that she is six feet tall.

7. We practice by shooting balls into a _____ .

8. The nets are hung around rings of _____ .

READ DOWN THE COLUMN TO FIND
OUT WHICH SPORT IS NAMED IN THE MAZE.

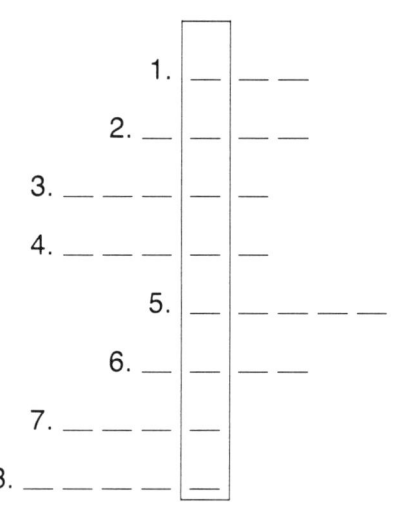

1. __ __ __
2. __ __ __ __
3. __ __ __ __ __
4. __ __ __ __ __
5. __ __ __ __ __
6. __ __ __ __
7. __ __ __ __
8. __ __ __ __

Which sport was named in the puzzle? Write it here: _____

Make at least [5] new words from this word.

HOMOPHONES

38   From *Make Every Minute Count*, Copyright © 1988 Scott, Foresman and Company

ANSWER KEY

In most cases, the "Bonus" answers will vary and there will be no "correct" answer. (Answers are provided in a few cases.)

COMMUNITY

FIXING UP A LOT

vegetables	children	build	flowerpot
cities	leaves	plan	row
seeds	houses	ax or axe	tree
flowers	squirrels	branch	bush

1. plant	2. garden	3. lot	4. children
5. tools	6. rake	7. shovels	8. hose
9. clippers	10. mower	11. ax or axe	12. garden

NEIGHBORHOOD TRIP
FLower   BRook
TRaffic   SWing
SLide   PLane
TRuck   SCooter
FRiend   BRanch

DIFFERENT PLACES
gerbil   gum
giraffe   gold
gingerbread   garlic
                  gorilla
                  goat

Bonus:
gerbil   gingerbread
giraffe   gum
gorilla   gold
goat   garlic

IT PAYS TO ADVERTISE
Beef   soap
cheese   rice
grapes   bleach

a	e	i	o
grapes	cheese	rice	soap
	bleach		
	beef		

SIGNS AROUND TOWN
1. pond   6. dump
2. cliff   7. bridge
3. bus   8. shack
4. craft shop
5. drug store

PEOPLES, PLACES AND THINGS
hotel   fence
bakery   club
signs   taxi
phone   swing

stadium   grass
sidewalks   college
babies   pets
policeman   hospital
station   traffic
slide   trucks

PARTING WORDS
de/pos/it	ill/ness	teach/er	ac/tor
tel/ler	doc/tor	prin/ci/pal	bal/co/ny
sav/ings	am/bu/lance	gym/na/si/um	stage/door

UNDER THE UMBRELLA
dinosaur   almanac   aisle
exhibit   books   fish
sculpture   catalog   juice
souvenir   desks   meat
skeleton   slides   mushrooms

| def | lmn | ghi | efg | rst |

ENTERTAINMENT

ENJOYABLE DECISIONS
price   camp
race   corral
pace   cable
city   cabin
circus   canvas
license   taco
celebrate   curtain
                  carrot
                  canoe
                  comic

SHOW TIME
let's
wouldn't
that's
aren't

1. wasn't	I've	was not	I have
2. I'll	don't	I will	do not
3. We're	wouldn't	we are	would not
4. I'm	you'll	I am	you will
5. Shouldn't	Let's	Should not	Let us

PICTURE WORD GAME
goldfish   pancake
flashlight   sailboat
streetcar   notebook
beehive   backbone

From *Make Every Minute Count*, Copyright © 1988 Scott, Foresman and Company

DAY TRIPS

1. Six	1. pond	1. drink
2. legs	2. hens	2. band
3. tramp	3. string	3. plant

LET'S HAVE A PARTY

sad	s
bottom	s
empty	s
open	l
cold	l
dull	s
left	s
big	s
light	l
stay	l

A WAY-OUT PARTY

OUTER SPACE VIBRATIONS
Enter: Jerry Blake's Launching Pad
When: Saturday June 3. . . . 12 noon
P.S.: Return Signal Requested

outer	out
vibrations	vibration
Blake's	Blake
launching	launch
requested	request

Moon Menu
Blast-off Burgers (Sloppy Joes)
Weightless Wafers (potato chips)
Milky Way Punch (chocolate milkshakes)

burgers	burger
sloppy	slop
Joes	Joe
weightless	weight
wafers	wafer
chips	chip
milky	milk
shakes	shake

CHANGING CHANNELS

mug	theater	clowns	tune
halt	youthful	untamed	flying
cooks	trek	exhibit	feast

FREE TIME

AFTER SCHOOL FUN

1. That's	5. isn't
2. Let's	6. I'll
3. Doesn't	7. couldn't
4. can't	8. don't

RHYME TIME

boy	boy
toy	toy
soy	
hike	like, hike
like	
bike	
look	book, look
book	
cook	

PETS ARE PEOPLE, TOO!

after	over
inside	tall
back	laugh
cry	delicious
slowly	happy
shouted	tired
started	warm
smiling	together

LIFE'S A PICNIC   YES/NO Answers will vary.

1. pear	5. won
2. for	6. bare
3. rose	7. write
4. know	8. would

CHARLIE GOES TO CAMP

tiny	my	Pete	great
me	lake	Wednesday	hike
climb	plane	stream	broken
day	soaked	place	hope

SEARCH FOR FUN

1. fishing
2. pretended
3. reading
4. painted
5. wearing
6. tickets
7. washing
8. finished

STAMP IT
1. fatigue-feast
2. vase-vein
3. attain-attire
4. crow-cruelty
5. expand-explain
6. ranch-rash
7. formal-forum
8. punish-purple
9. vapor-vary
10. hug-humor
11. neat-needle
12. respect-rest
13. position-post
14. antique-any
15. plaza-pledge

MYSTERY
IT'S A MYSTERY TO ME

s	footsteps	p	monster
p	robber	p	clue
s	scares	p	skeleton
s	spies	s	ghosts
flashlights	witches	captures	mysteries
grave	shadow	fingerprint	bone

1. bones
2. flashlight
3. shadows
4. witch
5. capture
Bonus: mystery   graves   fingerprints

BOOK BAGS OF MYSTERY
1. Th
2. Sh
3. ch
4. Wh
5. ch
6. th
7. ch
8. Sh
9. Wh
10. th

SOUNDS OF MYSTERY
The Hidden Treasure:

brook	book		
shirt		circle
soot		took
short	pork	
wool	hood	

The Animal Cage:

paw	crawl	
wood		stood
turn	curve	
huge		toot
autumn		auction

The Haunted House:

claw		paw
slow	load	
awful		jaw
sore	more	
group		loot

YOU HOLD THE KEY
uncover   questions   nervous   unusual
exciting   foggy   run   alive
caught   dangerous   skaky   scream

1. nervous   calm
2. safe   dangerous
3. normal   unusual

A MYSTERIOUS PLAN
1. robber
2. ax
3. trip
4. knife
5. dark
6. coffin
7. sob
8. spirit

THE CASE OF THE MISSING PREFIX
1. unlock
2. unsure
3. unable
4. unwise
5. unreal
6. unhappy

FOLLOWING ORDERS
List A:
2 magical   magic
1 magic   magical
3 mummy   mummy
5 mysterious   murder
4 murder   mysterious
6 mystical   mystical

List B:
4 Frankenstein   foggy
6 frighten   footprints
1 foggy   footsteps
2 footprints   Frankenstein
5 fright   fright
3 footsteps   frighten

List C:
2 ghostly   getaway
6 grave   ghostly
1 getaway   gloomy
5 grabs   glowing
4 glowing   grabs
3 gloomy   grave

List D:
3 skeleton   search
5 spirits   shadow
1 search   skeleton
4 spies   spies
6 spooky   spirits
2 shadow   spooky

STRANGE HAPPENING
journey (6)
opportunity (2)
patch (3)
return (4)
purchased (8)
arrive (1)
tattered (5)
fled (7)

From *Make Every Minute Count*, Copyright © 1988 Scott, Foresman and Company

SPORTS

DIVE RIGHT IN
1. permormance
2. accomplishment
3. flexible
4. dangerous
5. Attendance
6. visualize
7. careful
8. equalize
9. excitement
10. amateurish

SPORTING PREFIXES
1. dislocated
2. discontinued
3. preview
4. displeased

1. departed
2. defeat
3. depend
4. misprint

Bonus:
misconduct denote   deform
discover   prepaid   displease
replay   unhandy   rewrite

A SPORTING LIFE
Court:
receiver   center
slice   ace
gymnasium advantage

Basketball:
catcher
golf
singles
canoe

TWO IN ONE
grandstand   racquetball   flagpole
scoreboard   skateboard   gatepost
horseshoe   mountainside quarterback

(blacksmith)   horseshoe
(Hoofprints)   mountainside
(racetrack)   gatepost
(newspaper)   quarterback

STRIKE OUT

Word	Yes	No	New Word
1. bite	X		bit
2. shake		X	
3. plane	X		plan
4. blade		X	
5. note	X		not
6. plume	X		plum
7. huge	X		hug
8. spine	X		spin
9. mope	X		mop
10. slide	X		slid
11. paste	X		past
12. stripe	X		strip

cube   kite
robe   tube
dime   cape

SWIM TRYOUT
Stephanie was <u>interested</u> in <u>becoming</u> a member of the school swim team. She <u>practiced</u> her <u>strokes</u> everyday in the <u>swimming</u> pool. The backstroke <u>seemed</u> to be the <u>easiest</u> for her to learn. She <u>worked</u> <u>hardest</u> at <u>diving</u>. Stephanie <u>tried</u> to improve each day in <u>hopes</u> of <u>making</u> the team. At last, the list of <u>names</u> were <u>posted</u>. Much to her <u>disappointment</u>, Stephanie did not see her name on the list. Then, she heard her name <u>called</u> over the loud <u>speaker</u>. She went to the office and saw Coach Wall <u>standing</u> by the door. He <u>explained</u> to her why her name was not on the list. It was his mistake... he wrote the name Stephan instead of Stephanie.

1. interest
2. become
3. practice
4. stroke
5. swim
6. seem
7. easy
8. work
9. hard
10. dive
11. try
12. hope
13. make
14. name
15. post
16. disappoint
17. call
18. speak
19. stand
20. explain

THE NAME OF THE GAME
Tennis:
faul<u>ted</u>
<u>for</u>ceful
(de)feat

Baseball:
<u>pitch</u>er
(dis)appear
(in)field

Golf:
<u>season</u>al
<u>swing</u>er
put<u>ted</u>

Basketball:
(re)bound
<u>tall</u>est
(dis)tract

Soccer:
kick<u>ing</u>
goal<u>s</u>
head<u>ed</u>

Football:
<u>contest</u>
bound<u>ed</u>
(en)force

Bonus: basketball
        golf
        hockey
        baseball
        boxing
        football

TAKE AIM
1. buy
2. daze
3. pause
4. threw
5. break
6. main
7. pail
8. steel

b**u**y
d**a**ze
p**au**se
thr**ew**
br**ea**k
m**ai**n
pai**l**
stee**l**

Bonus: **baseball**
Answers will vary.

From *Make Every Minute Count,* Copyright © 1988 Scott, Foresman and Company